WRITING BLACK CHARACTERS

AN INCOMPLETE GUIDE

Salt & Sage Books

SALT & SAGE BOOKS

Cover designed by Blue Water Books

eBook ISBN 978-1-7349234-0-7

Paperback ISBN 978-1-7349234-2-1

*To authors doing their best to create a more diverse,
realistic, and beautiful world.*

PREFACE

As Salt & Sage is based in the United States, our readers and editors have mainly focused on African Americans for the statistics and references in this document.

The experiences of Black people vary from country to country. As an example, British experiences are broadly similar (e.g., comparable disparities in wealth, representation, etc.), but there is less academic research on it compared to the U.S.A. The first Black Studies degree launched in 2017, the U.K. census included ethnicity for the first time in 1991, and the U.K. has only officially had a Black History Month since the 1980s. For insights on how Black experience can differ in other regions of the world, see Chapter Seven, Blackness in Britain.

LETTERS FROM THE AUTHORS

Dear Reader,

Blackness is not a monolith.

The voices who have joined forces to make this body of work cannot speak to the entirety of the Black experience. We all have a myriad of life events that have shaped us, lived experience that we draw from. What you read here will reflect that.

This guide is intended to be a reference point so that you can be aware of various harmful stereotypes and negative tropes to avoid during your process of crafting Black characters. Even though things are completely fictional, certain aspects of your work will be rooted in real-world issues.

The written word is a form of escape. But for many of us . . . it's more than just words. Some situations will highlight our realities, so handle them with care. We encourage you to be mindful in your approach to both characterization and world-building.

Thanks for reading & happy creating!

Undrea

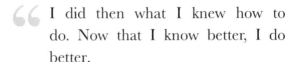 I did then what I knew how to do. Now that I know better, I do better.

—Maya Angelou

Thanks for taking the time to read this Incomplete Guide to Writing Black Characters. In mainstream culture, whiteness is the default. Your character can be overweight, have a mental illness, be a student in college, be an heir to a great fortune, or need to prove their innocence for a crime they didn't commit. By not making your character an ethnicity or race other than white, there's no need to see your story through an additional filter.

For instance…

- If your character is Black and overweight, could a potential love interest see that as a positive rather than a deterrent to love?
- How would mental illness be approached when in Black communities, people may look first to the church rather than a medical professional for help?
- If a Black student is in college, are they the first in their family? Was it a struggle to get there?
- When Black people pass down more intergenerational pain than intergenerational wealth, how do you explain your character inheriting a great sum of money from a family member?
- And finally, if the world already thinks you're a criminal, is it more or less difficult to prove your innocence?

These additional elements of characterization complicate your story. But that makes your fiction truer to life. The world is messy. We are large—we contain multitudes. Let that be reflected in your work.

Candice Roma

Dear Author,

Thanks for the effort you're making to read this book.

I want to gently remind you that while you might not share our skin or our experiences, you are still portraying them. Please handle with care. Remember that your words impact real people.

Thank you.

An anonymous author

WHY THIS BOOK?

Dear Reader,

Welcome to the first of Salt & Sage Books' Incomplete Guide series. We're glad to have you here!

Do you remember the first time you read a book and thought, "Ah! That's me!"? That ringing inside of being seen?

I do. As a child, I was obsessed with a Cinderella book. Cinderella was white, blond, and female, just like me. I was probably two.

As we interview for Salt & Sage, we ask, "When have you felt seen?" The answers we've heard from our incredible editors & readers have been inspiring and heartbreaking. Some of them have been avid readers their whole lives, but have yet to read about someone who looks like them, feels like them, talks like them.

In 2015 and again in 2019, the School Library Journal took a look at the children's books that were published in each preceding year (2014 and 2018). You may have seen the illustration—Google "diversity in children's literature" if you haven't.

The first time I saw the 2015 analysis, I came back to it again and again, feeling more and more discouraged. Initially, I couldn't believe there were so few diverse books. I started listening harder. Then I felt embarrassed that I'd been so unaware of the concerns (hello, white privilege & guilt!). I leaned in further. I tuned in to people who had been talking about this forever. I wanted to be part of the change with my own books, but I wasn't exactly sure how to do that. I felt nervous to try. What if I tried to write diversely, and I got it horribly wrong? What if I did more damage?

I confess, at first, I was motivated to learn more about diverse communities to keep myself "safe." That's a perfectly fine place to begin, but not a great place to end.

Fast forward to 2019. Salt & Sage Books was born basically overnight. It rapidly grew from there, and one of our most popular services is a sensitivity read. I'm really proud of the sensitivity reading services we provide, and of the superlative people we have on staff.

We've worked hard to create an inclusive, diverse, and safe place for our readers and editors to thrive. Salt & Sage is all about quality editing with kindness—and kindness isn't just an encouraging tone in an edit letter or complimentary in-line notes. Kindness is helping authors like you (like me!) who want to do better and be better, but aren't sure where to start. That meant providing a level of sensitivity reading beyond a basic rubber stamp of yes/no.

As sensitivity reads flowed in and out, I noticed a pattern: the same concerns were appearing again and again in the letters from our Black readers. I saw the same pattern from our trans readers. Once I noticed it, the pattern showed up everywhere: our sensitivity readers were regularly rehashing the same concerns related to their identities.

That got me thinking—if our authors were consistently having the same issues, could we

xiv   WHY THIS BOOK?

help in a more targeted way? And what about the authors for whom a sensitivity read is too expensive?

The more I thought about it, the more I liked the idea. I've talked to lots of people in the writing world about writing diversely, and the same thing stops nearly all of them: fear. They don't know where to start. They aren't sure that their Googled information is accurate. They don't know anyone who they can ask, or they are too nervous to ask.

After lots of brainstorming about the best way to provide this information, the Incomplete Guides were born. You're currently reading our *Incomplete Guide to Writing Black Characters*. This was written entirely by our Black readers and editors. They've addressed the most common areas of concern that pop up in their sensitivity reading. You'll see sections where they write from their own point of view. Multiple authors have contributed to each section. Some of them have included their names; others have chosen to remain anonymous for their own safety. (Doxxing is still a very real concern, and one we actively try to protect our editors against.)

As you read this, you might find yourself feeling uncomfortable. That's okay. Take a deep breath and lean into the discomfort. Remember that becoming anti-racist requires concerted effort and real intention.

Of course, even though this was written and edited by multiple Black editors, we called the guide *incomplete* for a reason—it's not a blank check, nor is it a rubber stamp. Even if you address everything in this guide, you should still seek input from at least one member of the community you're writing about.

Salt & Sage Books has sensitivity readers on staff. Many authors also have success posting about their specific needs on Twitter's writing hashtags. Be sure to pay your readers for their labor. Listen carefully to their feedback, and you will most certainly write a better book.

We hope that *The Incomplete Guide to Writing Black Characters* will be a helpful resource as you write diversely. We invite you to step inside the viewpoint of our editors and experience a deeper, more impactful form of researching. We hope that will help you confront your own biases when writing Black characters.

Mostly, we hope that you will continue to create thoughtful, nuanced Black characters. We hope that you will be part of the movement to create more diverse books. It's critical work.

It's occasionally difficult. It's deeply worth the effort.

May you write books that help people feel seen.

Erin Olds (she/her)

CEO, Salt & Sage Books

COMMON STEREOTYPES

A s you begin to write Black characters, it's important to take a look at the most common stereotypes. We will discuss ten of the most common here, but know that there are hundreds more.[1]

Be very aware of the following stereotypes when creating a Black character: Uncle Tom, Jezebel, Sapphire/Angry Black Woman, Mammy, Mandigo/Black Buck, the Savage, the Tragic Mulatto, Black Best Friend, Scary Black Man, and the Magical Negro.

UNCLE TOM

This term originates from Mark Twain's book *Huckleberry Finn* but has taken on its own very specific meaning over the years.

An "Uncle Tom" is a Black character (usually a man) who is servile to a white character, or to white society in general. They will protect the interests of the white characters or people as if they were their own, and may believe that following them or being obedient to them is the only way to function. This can also lead to them attacking other Black characters for not behaving in the way that the "Uncle Tom" thinks they should.

> Always as Toms are chased, harassed, hounded, flogged, enslaved, and insulted, they keep the faith, n'er turn against their white massas, and remain hearty, submissive, stoic, generous, selfless, and oh-so-very kind. Thus they endear themselves to white audiences and emerge as heroes of sorts.[2]

In some ways, you can think of "Uncle Toms" as tragic characters: they have convinced themselves that if they are good enough to white people, they will be safe, even though that is not the case. It is a sad and dangerous state of mind.

As a result, "Uncle Tom" is often used as an insult within Black communities when somebody is perceived as capitulating to white supremacist ideas, e.g., someone insisting on respectability politics ("if we all wore suits we wouldn't get hurt" or "if you're just polite then you won't get in trouble").[3] Be cautious when including this phrase in your manuscripts, however.

To avoid this stereotype, try to make sure that your Black character has a mind of their own, and is not simply there to support white characters.

THE JEZEBEL

The Jezebel stereotype leans on the assumption that Black women are more inherently sexual and aggressive than white women. It's a stereotype that supports the myths of rape culture specifically as they pertain to Black women, i.e., that they are uniquely and innately sexual, and therefore will consent to anything.

The portrayal of Black women as lascivious by nature is an enduring stereotype. The descriptive words associated with this stereotype are singular in their focus: seductive, alluring, worldly, beguiling, tempting, and lewd. Historically, white women, as a category, were portrayed as models of self-respect, self-control, and modesty—even sexual purity, but Black women were often portrayed as innately promiscuous, even predatory. This depiction of Black women is signified by the name "Jezebel."[4]

A "Jezebel" character is often placed in opposition to a "virtuous" and "pure" white woman character, and usually as a threat. The Jezebel might try to seduce the white woman's husband, or even the white woman herself. This is all portrayed as a kind of corruption on the part of the Black woman.

The history of this stereotype goes back to slavery, where white slave owners would make excuses for their rape of Black women (though, of course, these excuses were also related to the belief that Black people were not human at all). It was believed that because many African tribes were found in a state of partial nudity, they must be innately "savage" and "sexual," and on top of that, that the build of the Black female body itself indicates that it was "made for sex."

The Jezebel stereotype contributes to the "she was asking for it" mindset, but directed specifically at Black women; it is a specifically racist form of slut-shaming. Try to avoid implying that Black women are more interested in sex than "normal" women.

SAPPHIRE/ANGRY BLACK WOMAN

This trope relies on the idea that Black women are overly sensitive and easily angered for no good reason, becoming hyper aggressive and indulging bitterness about their situations.

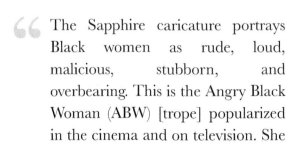 The Sapphire caricature portrays Black women as rude, loud, malicious, stubborn, and overbearing. This is the Angry Black Woman (ABW) [trope] popularized in the cinema and on television. She

is tart-tongued and emasculating, one hand on a hip and the other pointing and jabbing (or arms akimbo), violently and rhythmically rocking her head, mocking African American men for offenses ranging from being unemployed to sexually pursuing white women. She is a shrill nagger with irrational states of anger and indignation and is often mean-spirited and abusive. … She has venom for anyone who insults or disrespects her. The Sapphire's desire to dominate and her hypersensitivity to injustices make her a perpetual complainer, but she does not criticize to improve things; rather, she criticizes because she is unendingly bitter and wishes that unhappiness on others. The Sapphire caricature is a harsh portrayal of African American women, but it is more than that; it is a social control mechanism that is employed to punish Black women who violate the societal norms that encourage them to be passive, servile, non-threatening, and unseen.[5]

The key here is that the anger of this Black woman stereotype is always portrayed as unjustified: she is always hostile and overbearing, and sometimes gets her comeuppance later on in whatever narrative is being told.

This stereotype leads to the assumption that whenever a Black woman is angry, she is overreacting—and so the anger of Black women is dismissed. Worse, if she is angry at a white person—especially a white woman—she is deemed a threat.

Avoid this by making sure to give your Black female characters depth of character and showing why it is that they're angry, and validate that anger through your writing where you can. This doesn't mean "always make your Black women characters be right"; it means "show that there are underlying reasons for their anger that are not unreasonable" rather than just making them angry for anger's sake, or for a joke.

Give your Black woman character the space to be angry without being waved off or dismissed by other characters. Often, Black women aren't given the room to sit in feelings of anger or irritation without falling into the overexaggerated Angry Black Woman trope.

Black women are required to be strong 24/7/365, so, in turn, are often seen as both infallible and unbreakable. We aren't given the grace to display our humanity. Since Black women are pigeonholed into possessing other-worldly strength, we are rarely placed in scenes where we can be soft and vulnerable. This is true for Black men as well.

Make your Black characters strong because of their experiences. Give them space to bend without breaking.

To overcompensate for this trope, many creators will (unfortunately) make Black women bend over backward to accommodate those around her, regardless of the situation or her own personal emotions about the matter, effectively making her a doormat, which leads to the Mammy trope.

THE MAMMY

One of the most famous examples of the "Mammy" stereotype is Hattie McDaniel's character in *Gone With The Wind*.

Hattie McDaniel was a gifted actress who added depth to the character of Mammy; unfortunately, she, like almost all Blacks from the 1920s through [the] 1950s, was typecast as a servant. She was often criticized by Blacks for perpetuating the Mammy caricature. She responded this way: "Why should I complain about making seven thousand dollars a week playing a maid? If I didn't, I'd be making seven dollars a week actually being one." [6]

A "Mammy" is usually an older Black woman who takes care of white characters. In many ways, she is similar to Uncle Tom: she is deeply emotionally invested in the success and happiness of the white characters around her, even to the detriment of herself.

This stereotype is essentially used as a comfort blanket for the white characters: when they are upset, they run to the Mammy so that she can make them feel better. One good example of this is in the film *The Help* and those notorious lines of "You is kind. You is smart. You is important."[7]

The reason these lines stand out so much is because the person that these words are addressed to is not the person who most needs to hear them. Who is telling Black women that they are kind and smart and important?

The Mammy character performs this kind of emotional labor over and over again at seemingly no cost to herself and perpetuates the idea that Black women—particularly dark-skinned Black women—exist to take care of white people.

So, avoid having a white character constantly going to a Black woman for comfort without ever reciprocating. If your Black woman character does give comfort, make sure she also receives it.

Adjacent to the Mammy trope is the "Mule" Black woman. This woman is "strong" enough to be relied on to fix everything and take care of everyone. It's a really easy trope to fall into because it feels "positive." That doesn't mean you can't show your character taking care of people or fixing things, but be sure to also show the toll it takes on her. See if you can have her ask for help as well. It's important to show that Black women get tired and need care, too.

Make sure that you give Black women who have a caring role an internal life and personality separate from looking after others.

Mandingo/Black Buck

This trope is similar to the Jezebel, inasmuch as it assumes that all Black men are hypersexual and even threatening (especially to white women). In addition to being sexualized, this trope specifically focuses on violence as an inherent part of the "Mandingo" character—which often leads to this stereotype essentially casting Black men as rapists.

 This stereotypical representation has its roots in the racist doctrine of white supremacy, according to which those of African origin were marked as brutal savages, both mentally and physically inferior (facial features of African Americans were deemed ugly and apelike) to the white population; whereas, the very notion of miscegenation was considered abominable and unthinkable. According to the logic of white supremacists, the alleged violent, beastly, and subhuman presence of African Americans threatens the "ideal" white community, most commonly embodied in a body of a beautiful, fragile white woman. Evolving from the Gus character, the features of "the Black Buck" type usually include violence, rudeness, lechery, and disrespect for any kind of (white) authority.[8]

This character is shown as "savage" and "out of control," and therefore deserving of any kind of punishment. It's the kind of thinking that led to the murder of Emmett Till or any number of lynchings: that if a Black man so much as looks at you, it is an act of aggression (and in the case of white women, specifically sexual aggression).

This stereotype is most commonly found in pornography, where it is often a form of fetish for a white man to "allow" a Black man to have sex with his white wife. It goes along with the assumption that sex with Black men is in itself somehow more extreme or violent. It is an extremely harmful form of fetishization.

If you are writing a sex scene or a romance featuring a Black man, take care with your language so that you do not automatically describe him as overly animalistic.

The Savage

This trope is particularly focused on Black people who are directly from the African continent but can be applied to any Black person. It is based on the assumption that not only is a Black person automatically violent, untrustworthy, and incapable of reason, but simply "stupid."

> [In 1841, biologist] Frederick Coombs expounded a then-popular (and completely wrong) idea that the size, shape, and other physical characteristics of a person's skull determine that individual's intelligence. Coombs and his fellow phrenologists started with the assumption that non-northern and western Europeans—namely, southern Europeans (who were not considered to be racially "white" at

the time) and people of color—were inherently less intelligent than northern Europeans with light-colored skin.

Not surprisingly, this flawed premise led these Victorian gentlemen to reach a flawed conclusion: that people with heads that were supposedly more "apelike" in shape were less intelligent than northern Europeans and therefore in need of the "civilizing mission" that colonization was supposed to bring. The Victorian phrenologists developed elaborate typologies supposedly showing that Africans had the most apelike—and therefore most "savage"—skull types, thus justifying their subjugation under colonial rule.[9]

This is the stereotype that leads to people writing about tribes in Africa who attack anyone that comes by, or who suddenly betray people whom they have treacherously befriended. In short, this stereotype frames Black people and all of their various cultures as "evil" and dangerous to white hegemony. It is used to make the case that Black people need the influence of white people to become "civilized."

This trope comes up a lot in "traditional" fantasy fiction, particularly those stories in which a character travels from "fantasy Europe" to "fantasy Africa." It can also contribute to White Savior narratives, in which the white character solves the problems of the Black people because apparently they just weren't clever enough to think of a solution themselves.

Avoid this by showing diversity of thought and opinion in your Black or African-coded characters, and by fleshing out their cultures in a sensitive way (i.e., do not automatically portray something different as being wrong).

———

The Tragic Mulatto

This stereotype applies specifically to light-skinned, mixed-race, and/or white-passing Black women. It is usually used to portray a self-loathing character who cannot come to terms with their Black heritage because their idea of "Blackness" is entirely negative, and so they move among white society without disclosing their background (though they are usually then found out).

This trope assumes that if someone is of mixed heritage, they will automatically be depressed by it and wish they were white instead because of course being white is the best thing one can hope for (!). Often, this disconnect leads to them committing suicide—the ultimate tragedy for a Tragic Mulatto.

 White writers insist upon the Tragic Mulatto's unhappiness for other reasons. To them he is the anguished victim of divided inheritance. Mathematically they work it out that his intellectual strivings and self-control come from his white blood, and his emotional urgings, indolence, and potential savagery come from his Negro blood. Their favorite character, the octoroon, wretched because of the "single drop of midnight in her veins," desires a white lover above all else, and must therefore go down to a tragic end.[10]

This trope also runs alongside the idea of light-skinned Black women being more desirable precisely because it is easier for them to move in white society: the closer they are to white, the more acceptable they are. And so, in some instances of this trope, the tragedy of their life is that they are never fully accepted by either the Black or white community—the former because of jealousy, the latter because of racism.

It is worth mentioning that there is colorism in many Black communities (see the Anti-Blackness section in Chapter Six), which means that people with light skin do not share all of the same experiences as those with dark skin.

There are specific insults and prejudices against people with darker skin that light-skinned people do not experience—i.e., the idea that dark-skinned people are less attractive and more threatening. This means that people with lighter skin do have a form of privilege in the Black community.

If you are writing a mixed-race character, take care to avoid indicating that some parts of their background are "better" than the others or that they are especially marginalized more than others.

We need to normalize tales of people of color and Black characters who aren't wallowing in their circumstances as victims or martyrs but showing that they are capable of solving problems and overcoming challenges.

BLACK BEST FRIEND

This trope seems harmless on the surface—there's nothing wrong with having a Black best friend, after all. However, this becomes problematic when that's all this character is: a Black Best Friend who simply supports the white character, without a narrative or arc of their own.

As time has gone on, it has also become a way for some stories to appear "progressive" by including a prominent Black character; but the fact that Black characters are so rarely the actual main protagonist shows this for the window dressing it usually is.

> [The Black Best Friend is a] character whose role either A) revolves almost entirely around a white character or B) serves as a conscious effort for a white character/writer to appear inclusive.

> Simply being Black as well as friends
> with a white character
> does *not* automatically make a
> character this trope. A Black
> character who's shown to be just as
> relevant as their white counterparts
> does not count as this trope. Black
> characters with their own story and
> their own distinguished identity and
> goals are characters who undergo
> personal growth and [do not fall
> into this trope].[11]

In some ways, it is similar to the Mammy/Uncle Tom stereotypes, in that the Black Best Friend exists simply to support and/or comfort their white friend—and usually without any reciprocity. They often also die during the course of the story, sometimes as a self-sacrifice to make sure their white friend survives.

The essential problem with this is that the Black Best Friend is treated more as a prop than as a rounded character. To avoid this, give the best friend a well-rounded story and arc of their own, and make sure it's clear that they have other priorities in their life than their white friend.

Scary Black Man

This trope is similar to the Mandingo/Black Buck stereotype but leans much more towards violence rather than sexualization. This character usually doesn't have many lines other than threats: they are there to intimidate and frighten, and are usually cast as a dark-skinned Black man. Again, there's the idea of darker-skinned people being more scary or threatening; the Scary Black Man is rarely light-skinned.

> Note that the character doesn't necessarily have to be of African descent, just large, imposing, brown/dark-skinned, and have a tendency to make people wet themselves with a single glare. If a Black male character has other characters fearing him after he performs a certain action, he is not a Scary Black Man; a Scary Black Man has people fearing him because of his intimidating appearance. Despite some of the unfortunate implications associated with this

trope, some of these characters become popular because of how badass they are. The obvious subversion is to make this character not nearly as scary personality-wise as their imposing first appearances might otherwise suggest. Another subversion can be to have the character only act this way in certain specific situations—a man might be a loving father and an otherwise affable and easygoing person . . . who immediately turns into an enraged Papa Wolf whenever his loved ones are threatened.[12]

This contributes to the idea that Black people are inherently more threatening—you can see this play out in real life by looking up police accounts of why they shot innocent unarmed Black men. Usually, they claim that they were "scared" of the person they murdered, even if that person was running away, asleep, had their hands up, or was a child.

Try to avoid this by having diverse personalities among your Black characters; you can certainly have an intimidating Black man, but make sure there are other Black men who aren't intimidating so that you aren't creating a one-dimensional portrayal.

We very rarely get to see young Black men being vulnerable and expressing emotion. Just like with the Angry Black Woman stereotype, give your Black men space to *feel*.

Magical Negro

This stereotype comes up when the white protagonist needs help to achieve the goal of their quest: they need advice or wisdom from someone, and when this character is Black and exists only for this purpose, they become a Magical Negro. This is, of course, especially true when this advice is about accessing some kind of magic (or about the "magic" of self-belief or something similar).

You can see this stereotype played out in *Driving Miss Daisy* (Hoke Colburn, played by Morgan Freeman), *The Green Mile* (John Coffey, played by Michael Duncan), *Pirates of the Caribbean* (Tia Dalma, played by Naomie Harris), and innumerable other examples in television shows such as Heroes, Doctor Who, How I Met Your Mother, Vampire Diaries, etc. [13]

There's nothing wrong with having Black characters who provide advice, but if this is their only place in the narrative, their role is a stereotypical one. This is doubly true if they only live long enough to impart their wisdom before being tragically killed so that their words have even more importance for the white character.

So, try to avoid having Black characters whose only function is to aid in the white character's growth in their own journey.

As you can see, these stereotypes tend to fall into two main categories of assumption about Black people:

1. Black people are a threat to white people
2. Black people are there to serve white people

This may seem contradictory, but consider the history of race relations. Black people *had* to be cast as inherently inferior and servile so that white people could feel justified about enslaving them, but they also *had* to be cast as threatening so that white people could feel justified about all of the additional violence they inflicted on top of the slavery (though of course, slavery is inherently violent).

Try to write with intersectionality in mind—Black people are just as likely to have mental health issues, be disabled, be LGBTQIA+, etc. as anyone else. Regarding the latter, there is still a presumption that Black people as a race are much more homophobic than others—this is at best exaggerated and at worst false[14]. A 2018 report found that African American people are actually more likely than white Americans to identify as LGBTQIA+[15].

You may have noticed that a lot of the advice in this section essentially just involves making your characters well-rounded. If you're serious about honing your writing craft, this should go without saying—but because of the unconscious bias inherent in all of us who have been raised in a white supremacist society, assumptions are made about Black characters before we write about them at all. So challenge those assumptions before you write them.

1. This essay includes multiple stereotypes analyzed in streaming fiction (Netflix, Hulu, Amazon Prime) of recent television shows.

    https://pdfs.semanticscholar.org/6daf/d67540d-d1d1396b98080491ebb724c097786.pdf

2. https://www.ferris.edu/HTMLS/news/jimcrow/tom/homepage.htm

3. https://www.theroot.com/the-definition-danger-and-disease-of-respectability-po-1790854699

4. https://www.ferris.edu/HTMLS/news/jimcrow/jezebel/index.htm

5. https://www.ferris.edu/HTMLS/news/jimcrow/anti-Black/sapphire.htm

6. https://www.ferris.edu/jimcrow/mammies/

7. Brandy Monk-Payton wrote an "essay … thinking through what Black women feel while watching a white savior narrative—what I call Black women's simultaneous endurance and exhaustion," she said. "Another reason I chose this title because it reflects the racialized labor of care work, whereby Davis's character has to routinely recite this mantra to affirm her white employer's young daughter."

    https://news.fordham.edu/arts-and-culture/you-is-kind-you-is-smart-you-is-important-problematic-portrayals-of-Black-characters/

8. http://casopisi.junis.ni.ac.rs/index.php/FULingLit/article/viewFile/2303/1832

9. https://www.washingtonpost.com/news/monkey-cage/wp/2014/08/25/othering-ebola-and-the-history-and-politics-of-pointing-at-immigrants-as-potential-disease-vectors/

10. https://www.ferris.edu/HTMLS/news/jimcrow/mulatto/homepage.htm

11. https://tvtropes.org/pmwiki/pmwiki.php/Main/TokenBlackFriend?from=Main.BlackBestFriend

12. https://tvtropes.org/pmwiki/pmwiki.php/Main/ScaryBlackMan

13. https://tvtropes.org/pmwiki/pmwiki.php/Main/MagicalNegro

14. https://www.npr.org/sec-
    tions/codeswitch/2013/05/02/180548388/crunch-the-
    numbers-on-Blacks-views-on-gays

15. https://news.gallup.com/poll/234863/estimate-lgbt-
    population-rises.aspx

2

LOOKS AND VOICES

T his section includes some very basic guidelines for describing a Black character's looks, hair, and voice. Chapter Three discusses hair at length, and Chapter Four discusses voice in depth.

DESCRIBING SKIN COLOR

Err on the side of caution when using the word *colored*. This word has historical implications of aggression towards Black/POC people. If you are writing a historical piece where these words will be used, be sure to include the "when" of your piece quickly so that the Black/POC readers can prepare to enter the narrative with awareness for their own safety.

Avoid using similes and metaphors based on food to describe our skin color (e.g., "chocolate skin"). It may not seem obvious, but relying on this kind of description contributes to the idea that Black bodies are there for consumption (please read the essay "Eating the Other" by bell hooks[1] for more on this). The Writing with Color Tumblr[2] also has helpful discussions on this.

Remember that if you do not state what color your character's skin is, the default is white. It is important to say that your character is Black, but avoid food descriptions as you do so.

Biracial/Mixed-race Characters

If your character has one parent from each race, then they are likely to be very visibly mixed. It's much more common to be clocked as a Person of Color straight away and then ignored than for someone to think you just have a tan—your nose, mouth, and hair tend to give it away very quickly.

Of course, your biracial character can also be "white-passing" (see Rashida Jones or Keanu Reeves for examples of POC who are often assumed to be white when they aren't). Usually, white-passing people have a biracial parent and a white parent. Even then, the genes are strong; you might have very light skin but a full afro.

Personally, what I've experienced more regularly is not someone saying that I'm white but someone saying that I'm *basically white*. It doesn't seem like a huge difference, but it is. Being told you're white means you can blend in, that nobody would ever assume you were anything other. Being told you're basically white delineates a distinction between you and the majority. You may have mastered code-switching, you may dress to fit in, you may have otherwise assimilated to white culture, but because of the color of your skin, you will never be truly white.

The discussion around biracial and multiracial characters is so complex that it deserves its own Incomplete Guide (one is on the horizon).

Hair, Briefly

Hair is a very complex area for Black people, so the whole next chapter is devoted to the topic. It also fits into describing a character, so let's briefly discuss some vocabulary.

Please avoid using the word *nappy* (it has been used too often as an insult). Consider *kinky*, *curly*, or *coily* instead. Some exceptions are possible if the character using the word is Black, as many Black women now use the word "nappy" affectionately in an attempt to reclaim the word (think *Nappily Ever After*), but in general, avoid using it.

Before writing a Black character who you will be describing physically, I recommend deciding early on what their hair type is and how they style it. There are a variety of styles and hair types, and it's important to understand them individually.

You can find several YouTube videos discussing individual hairstyles—check them out as you consider the way your character will interact with their hair and hairstyle(s).

Try the websites Naturally Curly and CURLS for examples of what different hair types look like, and please see the next chapter for more details on Black hair.[34]

DIALOGUE

When writing dialogue for Black characters, don't use African American Vernacular English[5] or Multicultural London English[6] unless you have a very firm grasp of their principles, vocabulary, and grammar—and a good sensitivity reader to check your language. See Chapter Four on Language for some additional discussion on code-switching.

1. https://de.ryerson.ca/DE_courses/uploadedFiles/6052_Arts/CSOC202/Modules/Module_00/eating%20the%20other.pdf
2. https://writingwithcolor.tumblr.com/
3. https://www.naturallycurly.com/hair-types
4. https://www.curls.biz/curly-hair-type-guide.html
5. https://www.languagejones.com/blog-1/2014/6/8/what-is-aave
6. https://www.independent.co.U.K./news/U.K./this-britain/from-the-mouths-of-teens-422688.html

3

HAIR

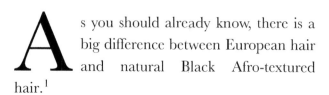s you should already know, there is a big difference between European hair and natural Black Afro-textured hair.[1]

We have to make and buy our own products because mainstream brands are harmful to our hair (which is why if your Black character visits a hotel, they will still have to bring their own toiletries).

This is why the tradition of Black barbershops and salons exist. The issue is systemic: training for many hairdressers lacks a module on treating Afro-textured hair. Unless these hairdressers seek out knowledge on their own (and often at their own expense), they don't have the knowledge or tools required to treat our hair.

We see clear examples of this in the movie industry—look up "Black actresses do their own hair" for several articles.[2345] Laci Mosely, a TV actress, explains:

 We've all cried in our trailers. I'm a dark skin actress in Hollywood and like 3 union makeup artist[s] know how to do my makeup and they're all busy as hell.

Everyone in the industry knows that there are certain barriers of entry when it comes to becoming a union makeup artist. Unfortunately a lot of the people who spend the most time with Black and brown skin find it difficult to get these opportunities because the [unionized] makeup and hair industry is nepotistic in nature. Friends are hiring friends, and when it's an overwhelmingly white industry, nine times out of ten, those people's friends are white as well.

This isn't specifically for vanity. It's the fact that systemic racism is so deeply ingrained in our industry that we are so forgotten about all of the time that this is normal. [6]

Carla Wallace, the head of hairstyling for *Black Panther*, also notes that beauty schools have huge gaps in their education for textured hair.

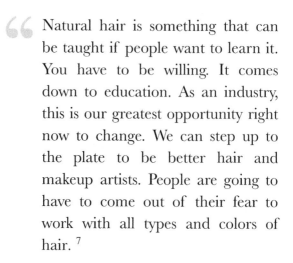

> Natural hair is something that can be taught if people want to learn it. You have to be willing. It comes down to education. As an industry, this is our greatest opportunity right now to change. We can step up to the plate to be better hair and makeup artists. People are going to have to come out of their fear to work with all types and colors of hair. [7]

On top of this, there is a huge range of styles for natural African hair. Some people wear their hair out, such as in an afro—which tends to be a specific, rounded shape like the Jackson 5 used to wear. Not anyone can grow one: you need to have the right hair type and have to let it grow long enough. The hair type needed would be a 4A, 4B, or 4C[89].

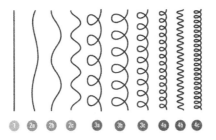

Others wear a wash-and-go hairstyle[10]. There are also what are called "protective styles," as they prevent our hair from getting damaged from too much handling or exposure to the elements. These include cornrows[11], locs[12], box braids[13], and Senegalese twists[14]. The latter two styles often involve three or four packs of hair extensions, depending on how long you want your hair to be.

This is a larger issue, but many Black women also wear protective styles constantly because they don't know how to style and groom their hair. Lack of mainstream exposure to natural Afro-textured hair is a real problem.

Combine that with the expectation that "profes-sional" or "beautiful" hair is straight and shiny, and Black women are often expected to use chemical relaxers to wear their hair straight. The natural hair movement has only really taken off in the last fifteen years or so. The lack of education about natural hair care (by Black people as well as other racial groups) is still a major hurdle for us to overcome.

Others rely on wigs and weaves[15]. For wigs, the person usually will cornrow their hair and simply place the wig on top (though the wig itself will require care to keep it looking good). A weave is simply an integrated form of hair extensions—there are many different kinds of weaves [16]—and can be used to create almost any kind of hairstyle.

Permanently straightening African hair is not a matter of just running it through a pair of GHDs. Many Black women and men are easily able to straighten their hair with just a flat iron, following much the same process as someone of a different race/ethnicity. However, the process itself may or may not be more delicate, as Afro-textured hair is often more delicate and fragile.

For those who don't want to have natural hair— and there are many complex reasons for this[171819]—there are chemical relaxers[20]. These can be incredibly damaging to a person's natural hair and often lead to Black women doing "the big chop" to begin regrowing healthy hair[2122].

African hair is very delicate and breaks easily, which is why there is a stereotype of Black women avoiding swimming.[23][24] The water will wash out the various products and treatments that keep their hair healthy, and salt/chlorine will dry it out (in the U.S.A, of course, there is also the historical issue of public swimming pools being segregated[25]). It is also why many sleep with headscarves or bonnets on—if our hair spends the whole night rubbing against the pillow, it may break.[26]

A common misconception I see is that afro hair is rough—the most frequent ignorant comparison is that it must feel like a Brillo pad. This is almost never the case unless the person has not been taking any care of their hair at all. Our hair is often extremely soft (which is another reason why we have to take such care with it).

As you write your characters, consider how they wear their hair, and why they might choose to wear it that way.

---

1. https://activilong.com/en/content/96-ethnicity-and-hair-structure
2. https://www.teenvogue.com/story/model-olivia-anakwe-calls-out-hairstylists-who-cant-do-Black-hair-at-fashion-shows
3. https://twitter.com/malcolmbarrett/status/1104802956296089600
4. https://twitter.com/YNB/status/1104947062649438208

5. https://twitter.com/yahya/status/1104468613422084096
6. https://www.hollywoodreporter.com/news/hollywoods-Black-hair-problem-set-we-ve-all-cried-trailers-1274876
7. https://www.hollywoodreporter.com/news/how-little-is-normalizing-natural-hair-Black-women-screen-1201588
8. https://Blacknaps.org/know-your-hair-type/
9. https://curls.biz/hair-type-guide/
10. https://www.naturallycurly.com/curlreading/curl-products/for-everyone-who-thinks-they-cant-wear-a-wash-n-go
11. https://www.youtube.com/watch?v=EmU5y8iKxNQ
12. https://www.refinery29.com/en-us/how-to-start-locs
13. https://www.allure.com/gallery/box-braids-hair-inspiration
14. https://therighthairstyles.com/senegalese-twists/
15. https://un-ruly.com/weaves-101-everything-need-know-weaves/
16. https://www.getthegloss.com/article/not-fair-literally-everything-you-need-to-know-about-hair-weaves
17. "Our perceptions stem largely from implicit visual processes, and as a result, our brains' repeated exposure to smooth and silky hair linked to beauty, popularity, and wealth creates associations that smooth and silky hair is the beauty default. Naturally textured hair of Black women, by comparison, is notably absent within dominant cultural representation which automatically 'otherizes' those natural images we do see — at best they are exotic, counter-cultural, or trendy; more often than not, they are marginal."
https://www.naturallycurly.com/curlreading/learn/theres-still-a-stigma-against-natural-hair-this-study-is-proof
18. "But the hatred of Black hair goes beyond ignorant comments. In fact, embracing natural hair can lead some women and men to lose their jobs or face punishment at school. In March 2014, the U.S. Army issued a new policy that banned traditional Black hairstyles,

including cornrows, twists and dreadlocks. The regulations even described these styles "unkempt" and "matted." After months of backlash and a letter from the Congressional Black Caucus, then-Defense Secretary Chuck Hagel reviewed and subsequently rolled back the policy."

https://time.com/4909898/Black-hair-discrimination-ignorance/

19. Assess your own bias around natural Black hair here: https://perception.org/goodhair/hairbias/

20. "By definition, a hair relaxer is a lotion or cream that makes the hair easier to straighten and manage. It reduces the curl by breaking down the hair strand and chemically altering the texture. Most women who decide to get their hair relaxed have curly hair who want it to be stick straight without any frizz. The results vary depending on your hair type, but usually a hair relaxer will leave your hair straight for about six to eight weeks. Unlike other permanent straightening methods, relaxing your hair will require touch-ups from time to time. You can go to a professional stylist, or you can purchase a hair relaxing kit to be used at home."

https://www.naturallycurly.com/curlreading/transitioning/hair-relaxers-what-you-should-know

21. https://www.byrdie.com/signs-a-relaxer-is-damaging-your-hair-400143

22. https://www.allure.com/story/how-to-big-chop

23. "African American hair textures are extremely fragile and when you add relaxers and various chemical treatments to the mix, it can lead to damage and stunted hair growth. Your natural strands will grow stronger, thicker, and longer without the interference of harsh and toxic chemicals stunting your hair growth."

https://www.kinkycurlyyaki.com/blogs/natural-hair-blogs/13-reasons-to-embrace-your-afro-hair

24. "Men and boys can hop into a lake or the ocean with few worries, but after the tedious work of straightening natural hair, who wants to mess everything up by swimming? Even advancements like relaxers haven't really helped much. If you spend hours styling your hair, or

waited all day at a salon and paid someone to style it for you, ruining your 'do with a dip in the pool doesn't make a lot of sense."

   https://www.byrdie.com/Black-hair-and-swim-ming-a-guide-to-healthy-locks-400048

25. https://www.theguardian.-com/world/2015/aug/04/Black-children-swimming-drownings-segregation

26. https://www.refinery29.com/en-us/head-scarves-alternatives

4
_____

LANGUAGE

C ode-switching is an integral part of many Black people's language.[1]

NPR's *Code Switch* podcast describes code-switching as "the practice of shifting the languages you use or the way you express yourself in your conversations."[2]

The Harvard Business Review explains further:

> Broadly, code-switching involves adjusting one's style of speech, appearance, behavior, and expression in ways that will optimize the comfort of others in exchange for fair treatment, quality service, and employment opportunities. Research suggests that code-

switching often occurs in spaces where negative stereotypes of Black people run counter to what are considered "appropriate" behaviors and norms for a specific environment.

For example, research conducted in schools suggests that Black students selectively code-switch between standard English in the classroom and African American Vernacular English (AAVE) with their peers, which elevates their social standing with each intended audience. We also see examples of guidelines encouraging Black people to code-switch to survive police interactions, such as "acting polite and respectful when stopped" and "avoiding running even if you are afraid."[3]

For Black people who live in majority-white countries, this means that they speak in different ways around different people (e.g., one way around white colleagues and another way around Black family). This is often to do with respectability—after all, because of the stigma against AAVE and MLE (see Chapter Two) as showing that a person is uneducated, you are likely to be looked down on if you use those dialects in a white workplace.

For Black people living outside of majority-white countries, we might code-switch from one dialect to another based on being in a professional setting (where often the bosses, etc. are white). Sometimes we may code switch based on presumed economic status, even within our own communities. As you write, consider the people that your character will interact with, and how they might change the way that they behave around them.

If you're not Black, you might be thinking that you also code-switch. While it's natural to change how you're speaking depending on who you're with, with Black code-switching, you must also take into consideration the systemic problems that require a Black person to speak and look a certain way in order to be respected— and in some cases, to stay alive.

Also, many Black family members also have a "house name," a name that only their family is aware of. It is primarily used inside the home. Typically, these names are tough to pronounce (to the native English speaker) and deeply rooted in their particular culture. Take great care when using one of these names for your characters.

For a book that deals with code-switching in-situ, *The Hate U Give* by Angie Thomas is a top recommendation.

---

1. https://www.npr.org/sections/codeswitch/2013/04/13/177126294/five-reasons-why-people-code-switch
2. https://www.npr.org/sections/codeswitch/2013/04/13/177126294/five-reasons-why-people-code-switch
3. https://hbr.org/2019/11/the-costs-of-codeswitching

5

FAMILY

As you write Black characters and their families, try to avoid the stereotypes of Black men always being absent fathers and Black women always being single mothers. This is a pervasive and damaging stereotype that is regularly cited as a reason for crime, especially in inner-city neighborhoods.

While there are plenty of studies that show that children raised in dual-parent homes reap all sorts of benefits, this stereotype ignores the systemic and radical racialized problems that lead to the breaking up of Black families.

 The conversation about Black single motherhood in America is driven by gender- and race-biased moral panic and is primarily a means to exonerate systemic inequality for America's problems, while leveraging age-old stereotypes to scapegoat Black women and their children. The reduction of Black motherhood to concerns about indiscriminate [sex], emasculating Black men, draining the public teat, and releasing frightening, no-daddy-having offspring onto beleaguered American streets stains every Black mothering experience, no matter how much individual realities differ.[1]

This separation of families has its roots in the days of slavery, when Black families were torn apart forcefully. Housing segregation, income inequality, educational inequality, and discriminatory hiring practices are all contributing forces to the breaking up of Black families.

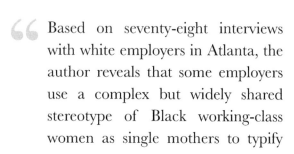

Based on seventy-eight interviews with white employers in Atlanta, the author reveals that some employers use a complex but widely shared stereotype of Black working-class women as single mothers to typify

members of this group. These
employers use this single-mother
image to explain why they think
Black women are poor workers, why
they think Black women are reliable
workers, and why they think Blacks
are poorly prepared for the labor
market.[2]

If you do choose to write an absent Black father
or a Black single mother, take care that you're
looking at the real reasons that it happens.[3]

Several news articles comment on this—Google
"missing Black father" or "Black absent father
stereotype" or "single Black mother stereotype"
for the most recent analyses of the problem.

As you're writing Black characters, consider that
there are many Black men who are actively
working to upend this "missing father" stereotype. The Made Men Worldwide organization is
just one of many organizations aimed towards
helping men with the "issues of fatherhood."
Founder Dennis Walton says:

 Our work is to help uplift men and
improve their circumstances so they
can become the strength they want
and need to be for their families. We

> decided to go beyond the local community, both nationally and internationally, to mobilize fathers, but to also restore communities through the restoration of fathers.[4]

Black families do tend to be larger than average due to the involvement of extended family members as well as immediate family (and due to people who are not blood relatives still being called *uncle* and *auntie*). Simply put, the definition of who is family tends to be broader—it's not actually a matter of having more children. On average, Black women in the U.S.A tend to have two children—just like white people and Asian people.[5]

There is a huge racial inequality gap in both the U.S.A and the U.K. This affects families as you may expect.[67]

None of this is to say that you can't write a Black character with a missing father or a single mother. If you do choose to include those characterizations, just be aware that they can quickly become stereotypes.

One way to fight this is to make sure that your characters are well-rounded and distinct. Black families are often shown in a negative light, so if

you can find a way to show their familial close-
ness in your story, that helps dispel that
stereotype.

Another way is to consider your Black characters' histories and the histories of their parents.
Look at the systemic racism and unjust systems
that have led to their situations.

Be sure that your Black characters have a
history. If you have a Black character in a high
school, for example, they likely have Black
parents and grandparents. Think about their
stories, too.

It can also help to trace your logic. If the father
figure of your Black character is missing, why
did you make that choice? Was it informed by a
stereotype? It's fine to start there, but don't stop
—make sure you consider the reasons, and don't
just rely on stereotypes to explain it. If your
character's mother is a single mother, trace your
logic there, too. Why is she single? Is it for
stereotypical reasons? Step outside of the
narrow confines of negative, harmful stereotypes as you consider your characters and their
lives/backstories.

1. http://mybrownbaby.com/2015/07/the-attack-on-Black-single-mothers-outrunning-stereotypes-carrying-the-burden/
2. https://www.jstor.org/stable/190387?seq=1
3. http://cup.columbia.edu/book/the-myth-of-the-missing-Black-father/9780231143523
4. https://apnews.com/725a00fbc56d4e71a2f66bae776cabed
5. https://www.pewsocialtrends.org/2015/05/07/family-size-among-mothers/
6. https://www.washingtonpost.com/outlook/2019/06/19/why-racial-wealth-gap-persists-more-than-years-after-emancipation/
7. https://www.nytimes.com/interactive/2019/08/14/magazine/racial-wealth-gap.html

ANTI-BLACKNESS

Obviously, most of this guide is to do with the effects of racism, but we should also look at anti-Blackness specifically[1].

Anti-Blackness is not just about the racism that Black people suffer in white-dominated countries, but specific prejudices from other people of color and within the Black community as well. The general principle can be summarized as the closer your proximity to Blackness (such as darker skin), the worse you are treated.

This is part of the legacy of colonization and slavery. The Indigenous people of the African countries invaded by Europe were told that they were inferior over and over again in various ways, ranging from forced conversion to Christianity to the Anglicization of their country's education systems to the installation of English as the national language. Those who were kidnapped, brutalized, and enslaved were told that they deserved it because of their Black skin; that their Black skin made them less than human.

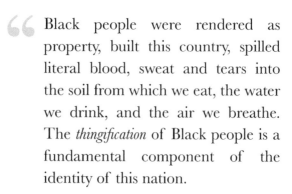 Black people were rendered as property, built this country, spilled literal blood, sweat and tears into the soil from which we eat, the water we drink, and the air we breathe. The *thingification* of Black people is a fundamental component of the identity of this nation.

Reckoning with this reality is significantly more difficult than wrestling with prejudice, racism, and even institutional or structural racism. And it does more than any of these concepts do to help us make sense of over four hundred years of Black suffering — of our unremitting interminable pain, rage and exhaustion[2].

Eventually, the idea of white people and white culture being "better" than their own became an unconscious assumption that was forced into the culture of these invaded countries and on to those who had been taken away from their homes (e.g., the enslaved Black Africans being forbidden to speak their own language or practice their own religions).

So people assimilated in order to survive and attempted to thrive in the new hierarchy that had been violently put in place in their own country or in the foreign places they now found themselves (e.g., on a plantation). Frantz Fanon put it this way: "The colonized is elevated above his jungle status in proportion to his adoption of the mother country's cultural standards."[3] The more acceptable one became to white society, the better one could be treated (and a similar mindset was embedded in other colonized countries as well).

 The logics underpinning anti-Black violence are inheritances of chattel slavery. These logics cast Black geographies as empty and threatening, open to occupation, and subject to surveillance and assault.[4]

Now some people who view things like speaking English as a sign of being more cultured or civilized will discourage their daughters from being out in the sun in case they get "too dark," and will view living in Europe or North America as an inherently better life—possibly without realizing that this life is only materially better because their own country was plundered in the first place. The physical and cultural elements that mark a person as Black are devalued, mocked, criticized, and minimized because Blackness in itself is viewed by people all over the world as lesser and as justification for violence against the Black person.

This is also why skin-lightening products are so popular[5], despite being so damaging[6]; why people often look down on Black men and women who wear their natural hair rather than straightening it or wearing wigs/weaves; and why people "code-switch" (see Chapter Four for more on code-switching).

This is the prejudice behind colorism[7]: people in the Black community who have lighter skin are seen as more attractive and "better" than people with dark skin[8]. The closer you are to appearing white, the more others put you on a pedestal. It should be noted that this is also a problem in

other non-white communities as well, not just
the Black community.

 Even for non-Black people with dark
skin, such as Indians and Filipinos,
some of the racism they experience
is rooted in anti-Blackness. There's
also colorism, a type of
discrimination in which lighter skin
is privileged over darker skin, that
exists among people of the same
race or ethnicity. Non-Black
communities have negative
stereotypes about Black people, and
these communities will distance
themselves in order to maintain
some level of power. [9]

It is sometimes seen as shameful to have darker
skin or very visibly non-European features,
because it is shameful to be Black at all, because
it is ingrained in cultures all around the world
that Blackness in and of itself is bad.

Apply this to your writing by considering all of
the sociocultural anti-Black implications that
your Black character is wading through every
day. Even if your book is set in a fantastical
world, remember that you as the author are a

product of our world, and have likely absorbed some anti-Black perspectives, even if you are actively working against it.

---

1. https://shadesofnoir.org.U.K./anti-Blackness-in-the-poc-community/
2. https://www.nytimes.com/2020/06/04/opinion/george-floyd-anti-Blackness.html
3. http://www.postcolonialweb.org/U.K./ishiguro/rodcolonize.html
4. https://journals.sagepub.com/doi/pdf/10.1177/0263775818805102
5. https://www.theguardian.com/world/2018/apr/23/skin-lightening-creams-are-dangerous-yet-business-is-booming-can-the-trade-be-stopped
6. https://www.glamourmagazine.co.U.K./article/skin-bleaching-dangers
7. https://www.thoughtco.com/what-is-colorism-2834952
8. https://time.com/4512430/colorism-in-america/
9. https://www.yesmagazine.org/education/2020/04/07/lets-talk-about-anti-Blackness/

BLACKNESS IN BRITAIN

S alt & Sage Books is based in the United States, and most of the sensitivity readers working on this text are also from the United States. However, much of what is in this document applies to Britain, too.

It is worth going into the specifics of what it means to be Black in the U.K. as well, as there are some differences to the American experience (though also many similarities). This section is written by a Black, mixed-race sensitivity reader from the U.K., and as such, we have opted to preserve the U.K. grammar, spelling, and punctuation.

HISTORY

The first Black people in Britain are thought to have arrived during Roman times—though there weren't many of them, they still existed. Several archeological discoveries have found skeletons dating from Roman times that appear to have African descent, including the 'Ivory Bangle Lady,' whose remains were discovered in York.

After that, one of the earliest recorded Black people in the U.K. was John Blanke: a Black musician who came to England in the 1500s and was a trumpeter for King Henry VII. More Black people began to appear as trade lines were developed with the rest of the world—some brought to the country as captives, others as servants.

Obviously, Black people faced heavy racism and discrimination; Queen Elizabeth I is on record as writing a letter complaining about how there are too many Black people in the country (though the number was likely to only be in the hundreds).[1] This can be taken as a given throughout history.

Technically, slavery was never officially legal in England; but that didn't mean much in practice, and many Black people were treated as unpaid servants (so a slave in everything but name). In addition, the country obviously still made huge profits from the slave trade and from using enslaved people as labour on plantations—and of course racism was (and still is) everywhere.

There was a boom in numbers during the 17th and 18th centuries, mainly because of the Atlantic slave trade, and the Black communities were most numerous in England's port cities (especially Liverpool, which was a huge hub for slave ships). The total population grew to probably around 10,000 during the 18th century, and it's important to note that these were not all servants, sailors, and other working-class people: Ignatius Sancho, Olaudah Equiano, and Dido Elizabeth Belle were all of quite high social rank. This is mentioned so that authors of historical fiction know that this was not beyond the realm of possibility.

When World War I began, merchant seamen, students, and soldiers from Africa and the Caribbean came to Britain (alongside others from the Middle East and South Asia), and racial tensions began to grow as they attempted to integrate into white communities. There were several race riots during this time. There was another boom in the growth of the Black population during World War II as people arrived for work to support the war effort (such as soldiers and munitions workers).

After World War II, the Windrush generation arrived. These were mainly Caribbean workers asked by the British government to come to the U.K. to help rebuild the country after the devastation of the war. They are called the Windrush generation after the ship (HMT Empire Windrush) that brought the first group of Caribbean migrants who answered this call for help to the U.K. in 1948. Then there was a second influx of immigration from Africa—mainly from west African countries, such as Nigeria and Ghana—throughout the 80s.

By the time of the 2011 census (the most recent census at the time this section was written), Black ethnic groups made up 3.3% of the population of England and Wales, with mixed/multiple ethnic groups at 2.2%. Combined, this is about three million people, with most being found in London.[2]

I have written this section because there is a pervasive idea that Black people were non-existent in the U.K. before the Windrush generation arrived (or indeed that there aren't many of us here at all). There has been a Black community in the U.K. for hundreds of years; you only need to read Shakespeare's *Othello* to realize this. I have also written this to show that you can set a book in the U.K. at many points in time and have a factual basis for including Black characters.

What racism is like in the U.K.

Obviously, there are huge similarities between how racism presents itself in the U.K. and in the U.S.A: lack of representation in politics and most other fields; race riots, police brutality, racist murders and attacks; and a lack of interest in repairing any of the wrongs committed are all shared across the pond.

However, one of the biggest problems in terms of racism in the U.K. is that most white British people are in very, very deep denial about there being something to talk about in the first place, and will immediately go on a fierce defensive if it is mentioned.

In the U.S.A, most people at least know about Martin Luther King and Malcolm X, even if they believe that everything has now been fixed (or, of course, are just outright racist). In the U.K., there is little acknowledgement of a fight for Black civil rights; in fact, most know more about Martin Luther King than they do about our own Black population. Many do not know, and more importantly, do not want to know, about systemic racism in the U.K.. They insist that there is a completely level playing field.

At time of writing, the leader of the U.K. Labour Party—ostensibly the 'left-wing' choice —has very recently called the U.K. Black Lives Matter protests a 'moment' and said that it was about 'reflecting on what happened dreadfully in America just a few weeks ago'[3]. This is a typical example of the attitude that many white British people—particularly those with more privilege—approach racism: it's an American thing, and not something that happens here. He does not understand or does not care that the U.K. BLM organization was set up because of things that happened here. His attitude is shared by a huge percentage of the population.

There have been decades of activism against racist policies, prejudice, and discrimination in the U.K., and a history of British racism could fill many books (and has done so—see the Additional Resources section).

For now, here are some key facts that will give you an idea of the atmosphere in the U.K.:

The first Black MPs elected were John Stewart in 1832 and Henry Redhead Yorke in 1841, but after them, the next Black MP was Bernie Grant in 1987.

The first Black female MP, Diane Abbott, was elected in 1987. She was also the most abused female MP during the June 2017 election.[4]

The first Black cabinet member was Paul Boateng, who was appointed in 2002.

Many racist political parties have been set up and attracted support, including the BNP, EDL, and U.K.IP; most of the time, they implode because of infighting, but there is always an audience for them.

The British Black Panthers were set up in 1968[5]

Jane Elliott is a notable anti-racist campaigner, and is most commonly known for her Blue Eyes/Brown Eyes exercise. Here's what happened when she tried her workshop in Britain: https://www.youtube.com/watch?v= Nqv9k3jbtYU (Pay particular attention to 11:20 —12:45, 21:10—24:20, and 27:44—29:05.)

In 2013, the U.K. government sent vans bearing the slogan 'Go home or face arrest' round areas with high immigrant populations. These were known as the "Go Home vans."

Current British Prime Minister Boris Johnson used to be a journalist. As part of that job, he postulated that President Obama had removed a bust of Winston Churchill because of 'the part-Kenyan President's ancestral dislike of the British empire'; said that Africa 'may be a blot, but it is not a blot upon our conscience. The problem is not that we were once in charge, but that we are not in charge any more'; and, in a piece about former PM Tony Blair, said that 'the tribal warriors will all break out in watermelon smiles to see the big white chief touch down' in an extended metaphor about the DRC.[6]

For every £1 a white British family has, Black Caribbean households have about 20p and Black African and Bangladeshi households approximately 10p.[7]

People of Black, Asian and minority ethnicity die disproportionately as a result of use of force or restraint by the police.[8]

The London Metropolitan police are four times more likely to use force against Black people compared with the white population. [9]

One of the most famous racist murders in the U.K. is that of Stephen Lawrence in 1993, who was stabbed to death by a group of white youths; the police initially concentrated on investigating his friend, who was a witness, rather than the racist gang. None of them were found guilty until 2012. In 2013, it was revealed that the police had spied on the Lawrence family directly after the murder to try to smear them.[10]

The McGregor-Smith Review found that 74% more job applications needed to be sent from ethnic minority applicants in order to generate the same success rate as white applicants, and that one in eight of the working-age population are from a BME (Black and Minority Ethnic) background, yet only one in ten are in the workplace, and only one in 16 top management positions are held by an ethnic minority person.[11]

One-third of those who voted for Brexit did so because they wanted to regain control over immigration.[12]

There's a common line that British racism is more subtle or covert than American racism, but in this writer's opinion, that is not the case. It is simply dismissed and avoided more thoroughly in the public discourse, and the victims are gaslighted more comprehensively. If you point it out, you are argued down vehemently because obviously Britain 'isn't like that'.

This writer's personal theory is that because there are proportionally so few of us compared to the white majority, and most of us are found in London, it is simply a lot easier for most white Brits to pretend that we and racism do not exist.

If you include a Black character from the U.K. in your manuscript, look closely at the political and racist landscape around them.

_____

1. https://www.historyextra.com/period/elizabethan/were-there-slaves-elizabethan-england-queen-elizabeth-slavery/
2. https://www.ethnicity-facts-figures.service.gov-.U.K./U.K.-population-by-ethnicity/national-and-regional-populations/population-of-england-and-wales/latest
3. https://twitter.com/BBCBreakfast/status/1277556165040148485
4. https://www.theguardian.com/politics/2017/sep/05/diane-abbott-more-abused-than-any-other-mps-during-election
5. https://www.Blackpast.org/global-african-history/british-Black-panther-party-1968-1973/
6. https://edition.cnn.com/2019/07/23/africa/boris-johnson-africa-intl/index.html
7. https://www.theguardian.com/money/2020/jun/20/financial-inequality-the-ethnicity-gap-in-pay-wealth-and-property
8. https://www.inquest.org.U.K./bame-deaths-in-police-custody
9. https://www.bbc.co.U.K./news/U.K.-england-london-44214748
10. https://www.bbc.co.U.K./news/U.K.-26465916

11. https://assets.publishing.service.gov.U.K./government/uploads/system/uploads/attachment_data/file/594336/race-in-workplace-mcgregor-smith-review.pdf

12. https://lordashcroftpolls.com/2019/02/how-the-U.K.-voted-on-brexit-and-why-a-refresher/

8

RELIGION

The history of Black people and Christianity is too long and complicated to go into in an Incomplete Guide, but it has resulted in most Black people in the U.S. identifying as Christian and the Black church having a huge cultural impact on the community. [1]

While it is too nuanced to properly unpack in this short document, writers should also consider the role that churches, especially strongly conservative churches, have played into anti-LGBTQIA+ beliefs. Many people belonging to the African diaspora have long-held beliefs about sin/shame. That influences their opinions of LGBTQIA+ people in a deep cultural way.

That said, it's important not to assume that all Black Christians will automatically have strong anti-LGBTQIA+ leanings. There are, of course, Black people who identify as LGBTQIA+ themselves, many of whom have also grown up in the church. And as with any other group, individual beliefs can run the gamut, from deeply homophobic to total acceptance and even allyship, depending on the person's background, experiences, and individual upbringing.

Also, don't forget that there are millions of Black Muslims as well—they account for a fifth of all Muslims in the U.S. alone.

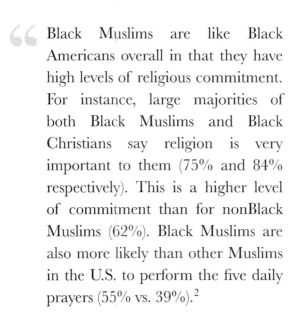

Black Muslims are like Black Americans overall in that they have high levels of religious commitment. For instance, large majorities of both Black Muslims and Black Christians say religion is very important to them (75% and 84% respectively). This is a higher level of commitment than for nonBlack Muslims (62%). Black Muslims are also more likely than other Muslims in the U.S. to perform the five daily prayers (55% vs. 39%).[2]

Many African countries[3] are majority Muslim (including Mauritania, Somalia, and Senegal). The Black Jewish community is also largely overlooked.

Finally, there's a growing number of Black people in the African diaspora who are returning to both traditional African religions and African diasporic traditions. Religions such as vodou, Santeria, candomble, and others that fall into this category are often portrayed as inherently evil, violent, or otherwise malevolent in popular culture.

> African diasporic religions are among the most maligned NRMs, largely because of Hollywood exploitation and anti-cult hysteria. This misrepresentation is doubly unfortunate because it has biased people against practitioners of these faiths while obscuring theologically and philosophically sophisticated religions. Haitian Vodou is likely the most frequently targeted of these religions. [4]

In fact, these traditions are complex, earth-based traditions that center around ancestor worship and reverence for the natural world. Their negative, and often amalgamated, portrayal in popular culture is largely due to racism and disinformation.

As you write your Black characters, consider their religion, beliefs, and how those will play into their character, their ethics, and their home lives. Is prayer important in their daily life? Do they attend worship services regularly, or do they have a more relaxed form of worship? If they practice a traditional African religion or diaspora traditions, please do the research required to make sure that these are not portrayed in a sensationalized manner.

---

1. https://www.pewforum.org/religious-landscape-study/racial-and-ethnic-composition/Black/
2. https://www.pewresearch.org/fact-tank/2019/01/17/Black-muslims-account-for-a-fifth-of-all-u-s-muslims-and-about-half-are-converts-to-islam/
3. https://www.worldatlas.com/articles/african-countries-with-islam-as-the-religion-of-the-majority.html
4. https://ala-choice.libguides.com/c.php?g=457246&p=3124874

9

AFRICA

I t's been said before, but it bears repeating: Africa is not a country. If you want to write an African character or setting, pick a country and research it first—the experiences of someone from South Africa will be very different to someone from Nigeria.

Take the time to look deeply at that country's relationship with colonialism. Did they fight in one of the many wars for independence during the '60s, or were they "granted" independence by an imperial power who didn't want to lose face?[1] Who were they colonized by—the English, French, Portuguese, Belgians, or someone else? What was the impact (for example, coastal countries in Western Africa were primary targets for slavery)?

Spend some time looking at the many different environments and geographies of different African countries so that you have some idea of the geological diversity of the continent.

The main trope to avoid has been mentioned in Chapter One (The Savage), but also avoid making comments about "primitive tribes" or "undeveloped" people—especially if you are using them for shock value or horror. Africans do not all live in mud huts in the desert—in fact, there are long traditions of advanced African architecture[23]—but even if they did, that does not mean anything negative.

———————————

COLONIALISM

A lot of fantasy and sci-fi novels and TTRPGs do essentially revolve around going to foreign places and looting them. The easy default is "go and steal things from these strange foreign people," but this can easily pave the way for the "Savage" trope. To avoid this trope, make sure that the foreign people are multidimensional. If they are hostile, why? What in their history has made them distrust strangers so? Be wary of painting any "discovered" nation or group of people a monolithic antagonist force, and not as sentient beings who have logical reasons for their actions.

In General

Make no assumptions. Research extensively, read #ownvoices stories from those countries, and find a sensitivity reader from that country to check your research.

Be aware, also, that if you are sending a white character into an African country or an African-simulacrum (in fantasy, for example), be very conscious of the White Savior trope. [45]

One quick tip to avoid that trope: make it clear that your white character makes mistakes—and that they *are*, in fact, mistakes. The average reader has been socialized all their lives to have boundless empathy for white characters, so what you might have written as their mistakes may not be read as them.

---

1. https://www.rescue.org/article/african-nations-struggle-independence
2. https://www.britannica.com/art/African-architecture
3. https://gohighbrow.com/african-architecture/

4. https://nofilmschool.com/white-savior-trope-in-movies
5. https://shadowandmovies.com/what-is-the-white-savior-trope-green-book/

10

OTHERING

Sometimes Black people take a backseat in their own stories, even when they are central, driving characters.

"Othering" is when a group or individuals are created to mirror Black or POC features, mannerisms, accents, and even traditional customs. But instead of having actual Black & POC representation, they are relegated to a non-existent group such as elves, orcs, aliens, etc.

In some cases, these fictional races of people are even impacted by historical events that have taken place in real life but have been altered slightly to fit the narrative of the main story and plot arcs.

Two examples of othering that have occurred in modern media are the Angarran aliens in *Mass Effect: Andromeda* and the *Na'vi* from the movie Avatar. Both are a collage of references to different races, but they bear no resemblance to the truth of who they are supposed to mirror.

This adds to the narrative that Black people are somehow "other" than human.

Diversity and representation matter, and they are vital. Othering an entire group of people isn't a tribute, it's a disservice to the richness of history and heritage that is present in the actual culture itself instead of merely being a hollow reflection.

Instead of "othering," delve in and research the significance of what you want to include. Flesh out the idea. Dig deep so that you can present something new about a culture and present it in a way that will honor the meaning behind it while also bringing authenticity to what you're creating.

Your work will benefit from taking the time to do things with intention.

11

INTERRACIAL RELATIONSHIPS

In current mainstream media, these types of couples usually revolve around one partner being white and the other being Black. Even in dealing with Black love and romance, the partnership still has a proximity to whiteness, but that doesn't have to be the norm, so don't be afraid to shake it up a little!

If you do choose to have two lovers where one is white and the other is Black, please be mindful that the Caucasian character doesn't fall prey to the White Savior trope. You want to steer clear of this if you can help it![1]

It can be so grating to read romance novels where the gallant, handsome white man glides in to "rescue" the poor, hapless Black woman from all her tragic entanglements.

Remember that your white characters do have privilege. Coming from privilege doesn't automatically make your white character a villain or vindictive, and they can even be unaware or naive, but be sure that they don't wield their privilege like a mace, intentionally bludgeoning everyone in their path. The truth is that privilege permeates everything, even down to the most "normal" decisions in someone's day. Don't ignore it.

Sometimes with interracial relationships—especially ones involving white men and Black women—there is an element of a Black women existing just for the sake of her partner without having her own autonomy. Often Black characters are pushed in the background, even in their own stories.

Part of the beauty of watching an epic love story unfold is witnessing two real people fall in love. Don't shortchange your Black character. Give her a full life and a full personality, and your romance will be all the better for it.

You can have variety when it comes to cross-cultural relationships. Black partners can have other halves who are Asian, Desi, Latinx, or a hundred other ethnicities! The potential of forming different, unexplored pairings can give a unique perspective to your audience.

Also, with interracial relationships, there is no need to have suffering just for suffering's sake. Undoubtedly there will be realistic physical, spiritual, and mental obstacles for your cast of characters to conquer, but Black love interests deserve happy endings as well!

---

1. https://en.wikipedia.org/
   wiki/White_savior_narrative_in_film

#WRITEDIVERSITYRIGHT PLEDGE

Join us on social media with your #WriteDiversityRight pledge. Tag us in your post—we want to hear from you!

I pledge to do my absolute best, do my due diligence, hire a sensitivity reader(s), and listen to and boost Black voices.

AFTERWORD

Thank you for reading our Incomplete Guide! We hope you found it helpful. Please leave a review so that other people can find it.

You heard from many of our Black readers in this book, and you've gotten a taste of what sort of people they are: kind, thoughtful, wise, and really, really cool. And best of all? They love stories.

Check out our wide array of readers at www. saltandsagebooks.com. Tell us that you came through the Incomplete Guide for a 10% discount.

You can find us on Twitter, Instagram, and Facebook—just search "Salt and Sage Books."

If you are a Black creator and would like to contribute to a future, expanded version, we want to hear from you! Reach out to hello@saltandsagebooks.com and use the subject "INCOMPLETE".

ADDITIONAL RESOURCES

American Lynching by Ashraf H A Rushdy

I'm Still Here by Austin Channing Brown

Just Mercy by Bryan Stevenson

White Rage by Carol Anderson

White Awake by Daniel Hill

Race Talk by Derald Wing Sue

Fatal Invention by Dorothy Roberts

How to be an Antiracist by Ibram X Kendi

Stamped from the Beginning by Ibram X Kendi

So You Want to Talk About Race by Ijeoma Oluo

Biased by Jennifer L Eberhardt

Me and White Supremacy by Layla F Saad

Uprooting Racism by Paul Kivel

Why I'm No Longer Talking to White People About Race by Reni Eddo-Lodge

White Fragility by Robin DiAngelo

Between the World and Me by Ta-Nehisi Coates

ABOUT THE AUTHOR

Salt and Sage Books is an editing company centered on the idea that a rising tide lifts all boats.

We are a creative community of devoted readers, writers, and editors, hailing from the desert's sunwashed sage to the coast's shining seas, and we've brought together our diverse skills and experiences in a single welcoming place, to help writers like you.

When you choose Salt and Sage, you join a creative community working together to change the world through story.

Check out our Incomplete Guides series for an accessible first step into writing diversely.

You'll find a wide range of editors, sensitivity and expert readers, and beta readers on our website, www.saltandsagebooks.com.

Welcome to the rising tide.

Writing Queer Characters

Writing Characters from the U.K.

Writing Characters from Spain

Writing about Anxiety

Writing about PTSD and Trauma

Writing about Therapy

And more!

If you'd like to see one of these guides sooner than another or have ideas for another guide, please email us at hello@saltandsagebooks.com.

Printed in Great Britain
by Amazon

46132887R00061